African-American Heroes

Muhammad Ali

Stephen Feinstein

Enslow Elementary

an imprint of

Enslow Publishers, Inc.

40 Industrial Road
Box 398
Berkeley Heights, NJ 07922
USA

http://www.enslow.com

Words to Know

amateur (AM-uh-ture)—A person who is not paid for taking part in a sport.

champion—A winner.

championship—A contest to decide who the champion is.

drafted—Made to go into the armed forces.

Muslim (MUZ-lim)—A person who follows the religion of Islam.

prizefight—A professional boxing match.

professional—A person who is paid for taking part in a sport.

Enslow Elementary, an imprint of Enslow Publishers, Inc.

Enslow Elementary® is a registered trademark of Enslow Publishers, Inc.

Library of Congress Cataloging-in-Publication Data

Feinstein, Stephen.
    Muhammad Ali / Stephen Feinstein.
        p. cm. — (African-American heroes)
    Includes bibliographical references and index.
    ISBN-13: 978-0-7660-2763-3
    ISBN-10: 0-7660-2763-5
    1. Ali, Muhammad, 1942– —Juvenile literature. 2. Boxers (Sports)—United States—Biography—Juvenile literature. I. Title. II. Series.
GV1132.A44F45   2007
796.83092—dc22
[B]   2006015872

Printed in the United States of America

10 9 8 7 6 5 4 3 2 1

To Our Readers: We have done our best to make sure all Internet Addresses in this book were active and appropriate when we went to press. However, the author and the publisher have no control over and assume no liability for the material available on those Internet sites or on links to other Web sites. Any comments or suggestions can be sent by e-mail to comments@enslow.com or to the address on the back cover.

Illustration Credits: AP/Wide World, pp. 2, 3, 5, 6, 7, 9, 12, 13, 14, 17, 19, 20, 21; Getty Images, pp. 3, 10, 15; Library of Congress, pp. 1, 11; Photos.com, p. 23.

Cover Illustration: Everett Collection.

Contents

Chapter 1

The Boy Who Had a Way With Words

Muhammad Ali was born on January 17, 1942, in Louisville, Kentucky. His parents, Odessa and Cassius Clay, named him Cassius after his father and grandfather. (He changed his name to "Muhammad Ali" after he grew up.)

Young Cassius liked to make up rhymes. His father worked as a sign painter. Cassius often gave his father good ideas for his signs. One day he came up with "Come on in, for a shave and a trim," for a sign for a barbershop.

When Cassius was twelve, he got a new bike. He loved riding it around town. But one day, his bike was stolen.

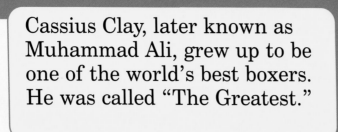

Cassius Clay, later known as Muhammad Ali, grew up to be one of the world's best boxers. He was called "The Greatest."

Cassius Clay, Sr., and Odessa Clay were Cassius Clay's parents.

Joe Martin helped Cassius learn to box. In this picture, he is teaching other boys how to box, too.

Cassius was very angry. "Somebody stole my bike, and I'm gonna whup 'em," he said. Cassius made up his mind that nobody would ever steal from him again.

Cassius went to see Joe Martin. Joe was a policeman who trained young boxers at the gym.

Joe told Cassius he had better learn how to box before he got into a fight. So he taught Cassius how to box.

Cassius spent long hours at the gym. He hit the punching bag over and over again. He jumped rope. And he began to box. The first few times in the ring, Cassius was easily beaten. But he kept training hard. Every morning he woke up early and ran for miles.

Soon Cassius was very quick on his feet in the ring. He began winning most of his fights. He announced, "I'm gonna be the greatest boxer of all time."

This picture was taken when Cassius had his first boxing match. He was twelve.

Chapter 2

Cassius Becomes "The Champ"

By the time Cassius graduated from high school, he had made a name for himself in **amateur** boxing. He had won six Golden Gloves **championships** and two national championships.

In 1960, eighteen-year-old Cassius went to the Olympics in Rome, Italy. He won an Olympic gold medal.

Cassius returned home proudly wearing his Olympic medal. The town of Louisville held a parade for him. But one day a waitress told Cassius and a friend that she could not serve them. The white owner said black people could not eat in his restaurant.

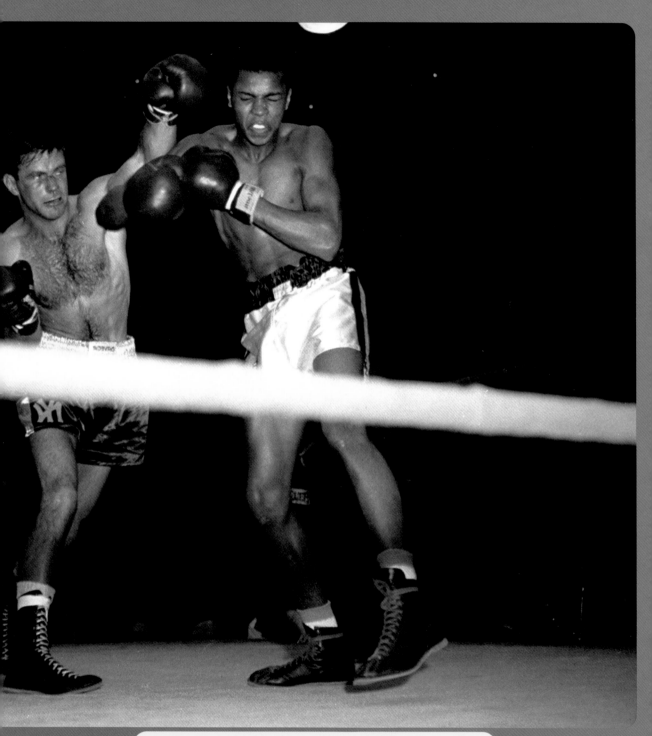

Cassius beat Tony Madigan for the
Golden Gloves championship.

Cassius was very proud when he won an Olympic gold medal.

This restaurant would not serve food to black people. This happened to Cassius, too.

Cassius knew that African Americans were fighting to get the same rights as white people. He, too, would take part in that fight.

Shortly after the Olympics, Cassius became a **professional** boxer. Now he would be paid when he won fights. He won one **prizefight** after another.

Cassius liked to work out in the gym
with his brother, Rudy (on left).

Cassius had a way of moving quickly when he boxed, almost like dancing. He was so quick that other fighters had trouble landing a punch. Then Cassius would swoop in with a powerful super-fast left jab that hit its mark. "I float like a butterfly and sting like a bee," said Cassius.

In February 1964, Cassius became world heavyweight **champion** when he beat Sonny Liston.

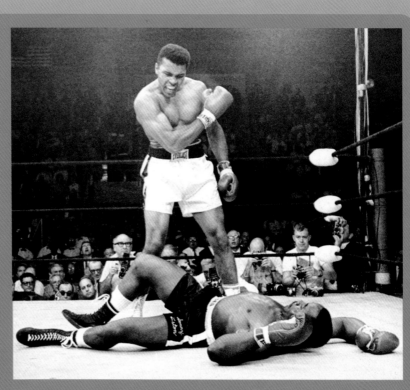

Cassius knocked out Sonny Liston and became the champion.

Chapter 3
Cassius Changes His Name

Soon after his fight with Liston, Cassius announced that he had become a **Muslim**. He took the Muslim name Muhammad Ali.

Over the next three years, Ali held onto his title by winning eight fights.

In this picture, Muhammad Ali is speaking to a meeting of American Muslims.

Ali trained hard to hold onto his title.

In 1967, Ali got into a different kind of fight. This was a fight with the United States government. At the time, America was at war in a country called Vietnam. Many young men were being **drafted**, or made to join the army.

One day Ali got a notice that he was being drafted. But he thought America should not be fighting in Vietnam. Ali said he would not join the army because of his religion.

Many Americans who had been fans of Ali now turned against him. They called him bad names. Ali was arrested and put on trial. In June 1967, a jury said Ali would have to spend five years in jail and pay a $10,000 fine.

The World Boxing Association took away Ali's title. Many states would not let Ali box.

In this picture, Muhammad Ali is going into the draft office to say he will not fight in the Army.

Chapter 4

Ali Wins Back His Title

Muhammad Ali waited for the court to hear his case again. He kept speaking out against the war. He went to colleges all across the country talking to the students. Some people liked Ali for standing up for what he believed.

In 1970, Joe Frazier became the new heavyweight champion without having to fight Ali. By now many Americans had turned against the war.

In 1971, the U.S. Supreme Court said that Ali was not guilty. He did not have to go to jail or pay the fine. He was now free to box again.

Many people thought that what Muhammad Ali was saying and doing was right.

Muhammad Ali became the champion again when he beat George Foreman.

Ali fought Frazier and lost, but he won his next two fights with Frazier. But by now, George Foreman had taken the title from Frazier. So in 1974, Ali fought Foreman, knocked him out, and became the champ again. In 1978 Ali beat Leon Spinks. He was the first person ever to win the heavyweight boxing title three times.

Ali retired from boxing in 1981. In 1996, he lit the Olympic torch at the opening of the Summer Olympics in Atlanta, Georgia. At the time, he had an illness that made him shake and move slowly. But to his millions of fans around the world, Muhammad Ali will always be "The Greatest."

Ali's Own Words

"Champions aren't made in gyms. Champions are made from something they have deep inside them: a desire, a dream, a vision."

Timeline

1942—Cassius Clay is born in Louisville, Kentucky, on January 17.

1960—Cassius wins an Olympic gold medal in Rome, Italy.

1964—Cassius wins the World Heavyweight Championship title in a fight against Sonny Liston. He becomes a Muslim and takes the name Muhammad Ali.

1967—Ali says he will not join the army. He is sentenced to five years in jail and fined $10,000. His title is taken away.

1971—The U.S. Supreme Court says Ali is not guilty. Ali begins boxing again.

1974—Ali knocks out George Foreman and gets back the World Heavyweight Championship title.

1978—Ali beats Leon Spinks. He becomes the first heavyweight boxer to win the title three times.

1981—Ali retires from boxing.

Learn More

Books

Bolden, Tonya. *The Champ: The Story of Muhammad Ali*. New York: Alfred A. Knopf, 2004.

Brown, Jonatha A. *Muhammad Ali*. Milwaukee, Wisc.: Weekly Reader Early Learning Library, 2006.

Haskins, Jim. *Champion: The Story of Muhammad Ali*. New York: Walker Books, 2002.

Web Sites

Muhammad Ali
<http://www.ali.com>

Muhammad Ali Center: Cultural Buzz
<http://www.alicenter.org/culturalbuzz>

Index

HSTAX +
        B
        A398F

FEINSTEIN, STEPHEN.
    MUHAMMAD ALI

STANAKER
06/07